Reading Roundabout

I am a Sikh

James Nixon

Photography by Chris Fairclough

W
FRANKLIN WATTS
LONDON • SYDNEY

First published in 2007 by
Franklin Watts
338 Euston Road
London NW1 3BH

Franklin Watts Australia
Level 17/207 Kent Street
Sydney NSW 2000

ISBN: 978 0 7496 7447 2 (hbk)
ISBN: 978 0 7496 7459 5 (pbk)

Dewey classification number: 294.6

A CIP catalogue record for this book is available from the British Library.

Planning and production by Discovery Books Limited
Editor: James Nixon
Designer: Ian Winton
Photography: Chris Fairclough
Series advisors: Diana Bentley MA and Dee Reid MA,
Fellows of Oxford Brookes University

The author, packager and publisher would like to thank the following people for their participation in this book: Jeevan Singh and Manjit Kaur and family; Gurdwara Singh Sabha, Bradford.

All photographs by Chris Fairclough except for p. 20: Philipp Maitz/istockphoto.com.

Printed in China

Franklin Watts is a division of Hachette Children's books,
an Hachette Livre UK company.

Contents

79 701 405 1

I am a Sikh

My name is Jeevan and I am a Sikh.

Sikhs believe in God and worship him.

Wearing a turban

I wear a patka to show that I am a Sikh.

When I am older
I will wear a turban
like Dad.

Worshipping

Sikhs worship God in many ways. We play holy music.

We worship God together at the gurdwara.

Showing respect

At the gurdwara we take off our shoes.

We bow to the holy book. Then it is read to us.

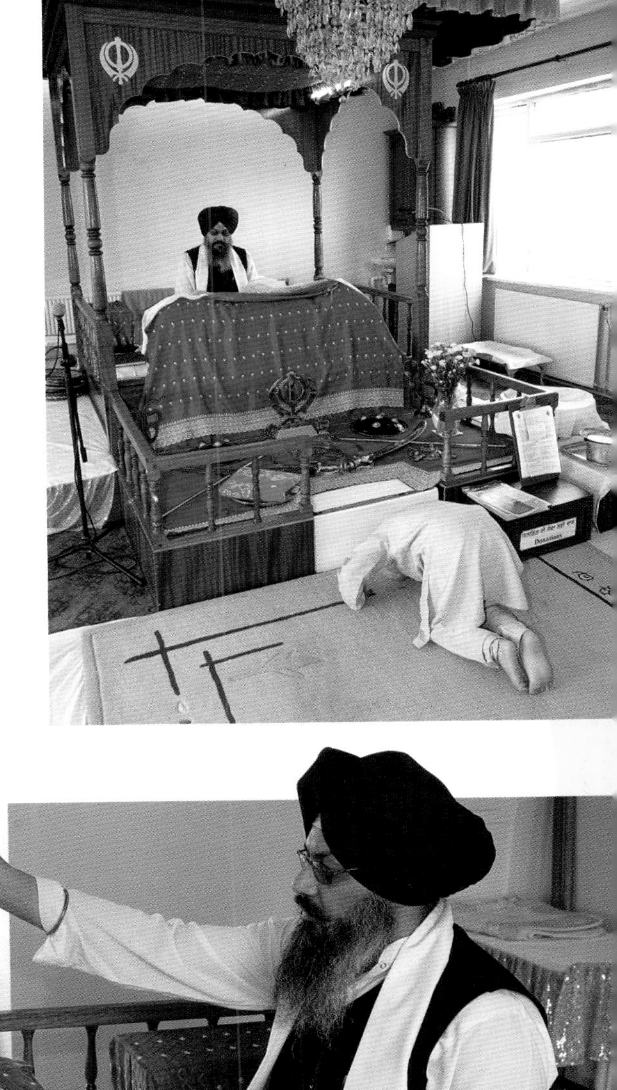

The Guru Granth Sahib

Our holy book has poems that teach us about God.

Guru Granth Sahib

Guru Nanak

Many were written by Guru Nanak. He was the first Sikh teacher.

Sharing a meal

After worship we all share a meal.

We are also given a special sweet pudding.

Living as a Sikh

As Sikhs we like to work hard.

We help people and share with others.

Praying to God

At home I read prayers from my prayer book.

My beads help me think about God.

Festivals

Sikhs have many festivals. At Diwali we have fireworks.

Vaisakhi is our harvest festival. It's very colourful.

God is good

I am happy to be a Sikh.

God is really
good to me.

Word bank

Look back for these words and pictures.

Beads

Diwali

Gurdwara

Guru Granth Sahib

Guru Nanak

Music

Patka

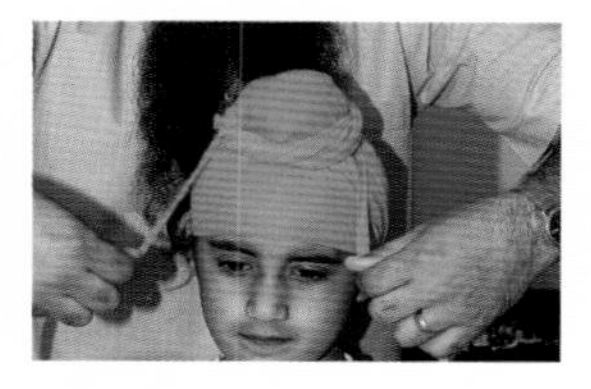

Prayer book

Share

Turban

Vaisakhi

Worship